Who is a Mother?
by Anna Nadler

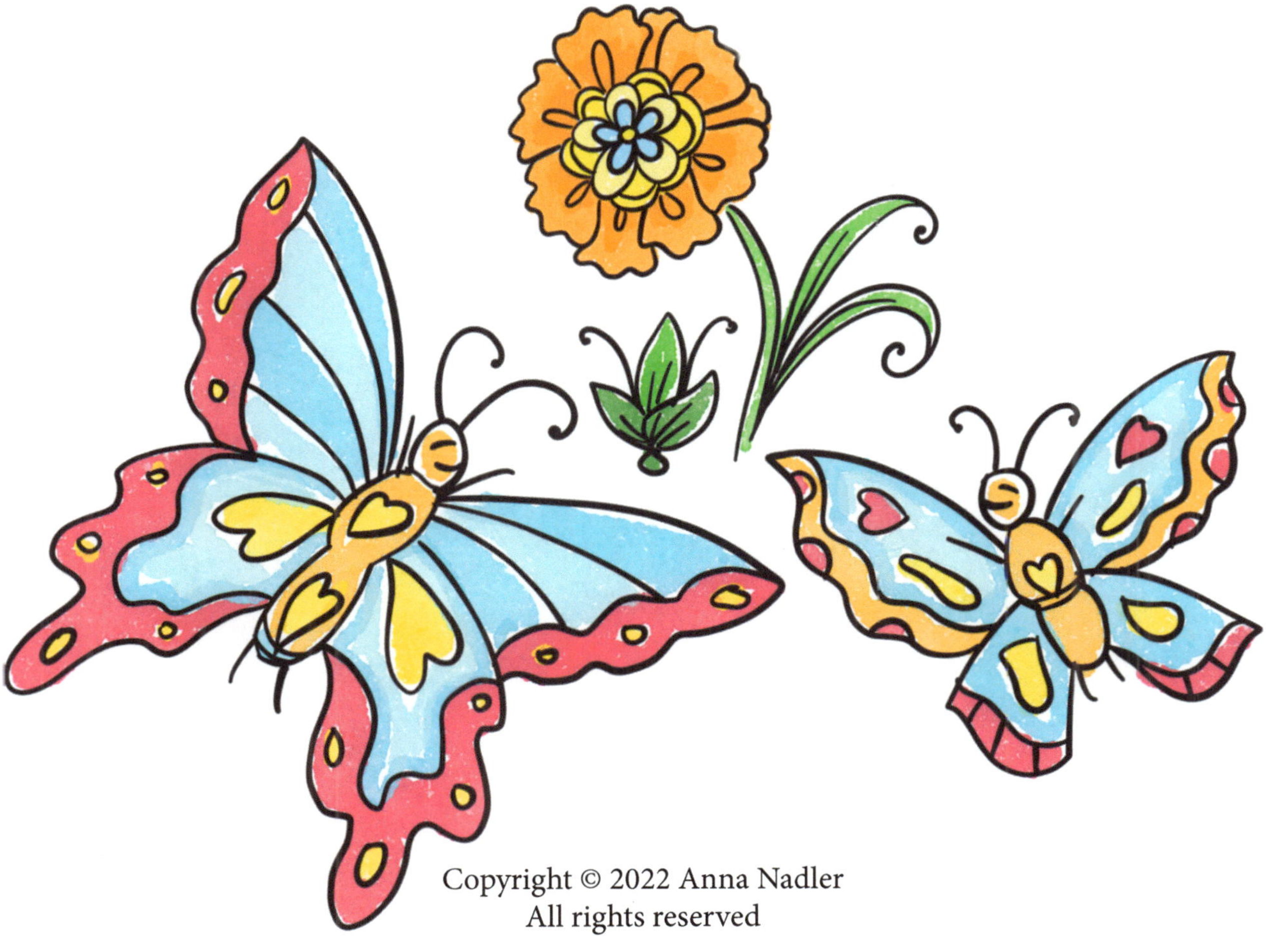

ISBN: 9781958428191

A mother's a person,

Who grows your life

She's there for you

In glory and strife

She'll make you tea

Or bake you a pie

She'll listen to you

As you whine and cry

A mother's a person

Who walks with you

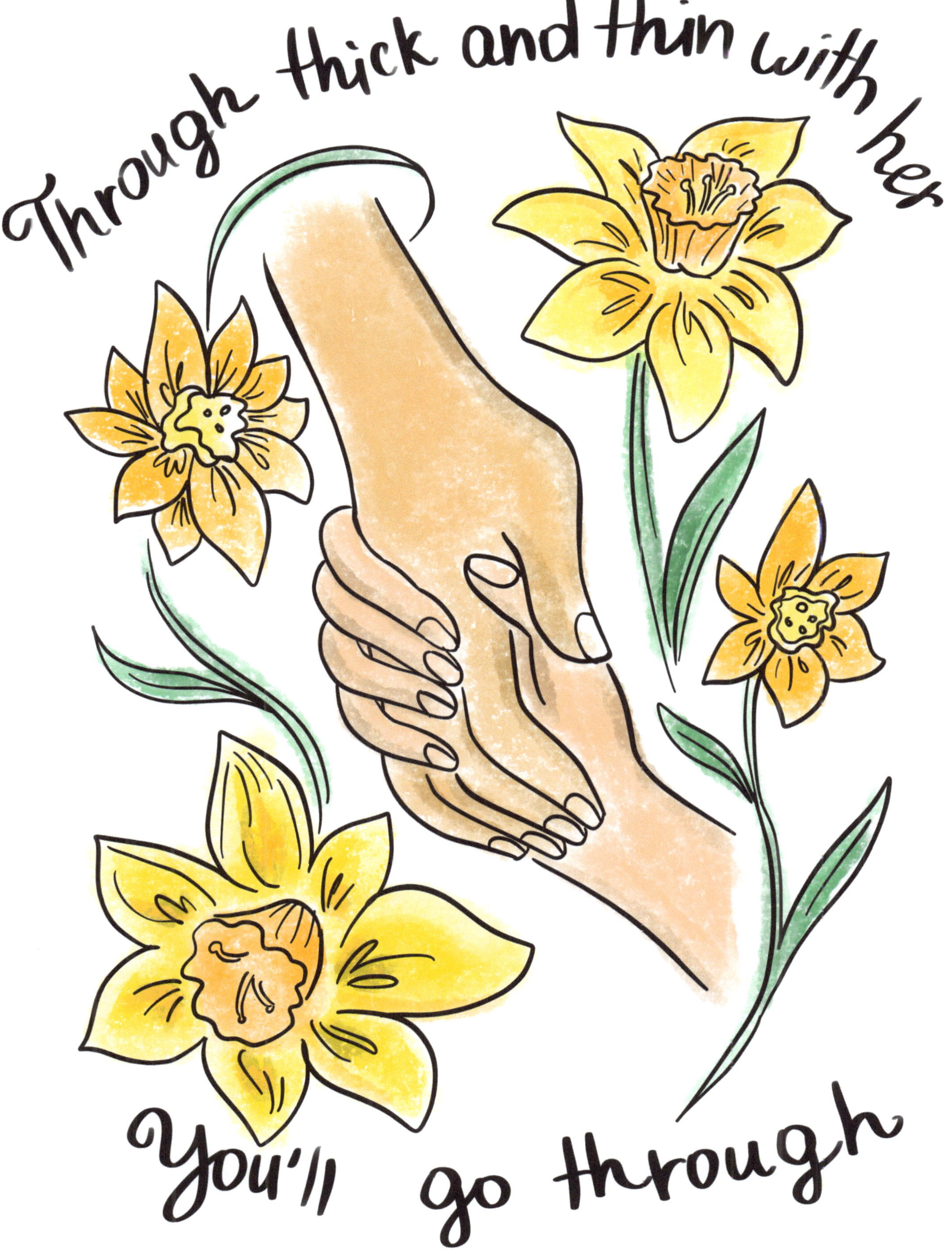
Through thick and thin with her
You'll go through

Though skies may darken

With wind and gloom

You'll both rejoice

When the flowers bloom

A mother's a person

Who always supports

No matter what ailment

LOVE

JOY

Care

No matter what hurts

A mother's a person

Who won't hold a grudge

Nor spend lots of time

To belittle and judge

A mother's a person

Who likes to laugh

Wears a good sence of humor

Like a flowery scarf

She wears funky boots

And wide overalls

She likes to draw

Or knit, or crochet

To sew, or garden

Or papier mâché

Her hobbies range

From dancing to hiking

Some moms are into

Mountain biking !

Because she's a person

Who's found her spot

At work and at home

She is lively and peppy

May she always flourish,

Be healthy & happy!

But don't forget...

A mother's a person
who has her flaws –
Sometimes she gets angry
Just because...

Sometimes she feels GLAD or MAD and SAD

Expressing emotion
Is not so bad...

We may want our mother
To be   Ideal

But she's only human
And she is real

About the Author

Anna Nadler is an illustrator, graphic designer and author, who lives and works in Staten Island, NY. She loves drawing people, fashion, animals and architecture - trying to capture the unique feeling of every subject she illustrates.

She is always working on new children's books, activity books, coloring books and more.

You can find Anna's books on Amazon and other book retailers. See more of Anna's illustrations, books, paintings, logo designs, and products on her website - AnnaNadlerArt.com.